This book belongs to:

_____

_____

_____

12 Months to Happier Habits

Journaling exercises to explore habits, triggers, and coping skills leading to a happier version of you.

Written by Dr. Kendal Maxwell
Clinical Neuropsychologist

Design by Victoria Nicole Varela

To my family and friends, for always reminding me that consistency is the key to a good quality of life. Thank you for always supporting me on my journeys to develop a better understanding of myself and in turn to be able to help others more effectively.

"Your net worth to the world is usually determined by what remains after your bad habits are subtracted from your good ones."
-Benjamin Franklin

As humans, we have all developed habits that can hold us back from achieving our full potential within our lives. Understanding ourselves and our patterns of behavior can create insight into why we do what we do and why we feel what we feel. While some habits propel us forward, others can work against us and hold us back. Developing the ability to identify self limiting habits can lead us toward incorporating habits that will lead us to success.

With each behavior we have, we need to spend time thinking about how it affects our lives; analyzing it. And we need to challenge ourselves to see if modifying it or even eliminating it will improve the quality of our life. It can feel daunting to spend time exploring a habit from the ground up; however, by taking one day at a time to review how things went can be eye opening. By analyzing and challenging our day to day habits we begin to recognize what can lead to more lasting change. This process allows us to develop new goals for ourselves and lead us toward our full potential.

This journal is a year long commitment to 12 habits, one per month. You will decide to either remove a habit or add a habit each month. You will explore what comes up. What coping skills can you think about before the month starts that will help you achieve your goal? What triggers do you notice as the weeks go on and how do you deal with them when they occur during this challenge? If you do not follow through, can you challenge yourself to focus on the events of that day/time and make a goal to get back on track while also giving yourself grace that this is just a learning point for you?

At the end of each month set aside time to focus on what your goal for each habit will be moving forward. Check back in with yourself each additional month thereafter to see if you continue to honor your new relationship with this habit. Explore what got in the way if you fell off track, and consider how you may be able to change your goal so it is more achievable if you need to. We all have things we wish we did more or less of in our lives. Now is the time to explore this without judgment.

This challenge is about beginning to understand your relationship with each habit and how to modify it to work to your advantage. It's not about eliminating unhealthy habits or forcing yourself to do an activity daily forever; rather, it's about beginning to understand your relationship with each habit and how to make it work better so you can be the optimal version of yourself. Start by eliminating habits you find are holding you back, then begin working on habits you want to add towards the end of your journey. I want each of you to know I came up with the concept of the journal during the pandemic and I guinea pigged it during that time. It has truly impacted my life and my view of my habits and I hope it is just as impactful for you. The following pages are some general lists of habits people tend to want to give up or start to lead a more balanced life. It is not exhaustive, but will hopefully allow you to explore for yourself 12 habits to choose. The rest of the pages are devoted to your personal journey. Good luck and I wish you happier habits from this challenge!

With loving kindness,

Dr. Kendal Maxwell

Contents

Sample List of Habits to Attempt Eliminating
Months 1-6

nail biting, sleeping in, smoking, drinking, drugs,
coffee, eating fast food, eating meat, eating out,
drinking soda, eating artificial sugar or candy, eating carbs,
chewing gum, eating past a certain time of day,
eating food groups you wish to eliminate,
eating with mouth open, picking at teeth,
shopping, checking social media, watching tv, swearing,
talking to yourself, responding to work calls after hours,
pulling or picking at hair or nails, playing video games,
engaging in a negative relationship, leaving work on time,
being on your phone certain hours or amount of time,
being late to meetings/outings,
sleeping with mouth open, sleeping in contacts,
sitting too long, cracking joints, driving too fast, biting
your lip or cheek, pornography, watching the news,
interrupting others when talking, engaging in negative
self-talk, eliminating certain words like um and uh, cursing,
gambling, whining, littering, leaving clothes out of place,
texting and driving, leaving lights or devices on, gossiping,
lying, criticizing others, rolling your eyes, invading personal
space, clicking or biting pen/pencils, talking too fast,
popping pimples...

Sample List of Habits to Introduce
Months 7-12

meditation, exercising/walking, going outdoors,

engaging in a new sport, stretching, improving posture,

making plans to see others outside of house,

calling people you love, acts of kindness towards others,

journaling, expressing gratitude, playing an instrument,

reading a book,washing hands correctly, flossing teeth,

brushing teeth regularly, washing face, taking vitamins or

medications consistently, cleaning up, keeping organized,

increasing eye contact, smiling, saying please more,

learning a new language, learning a new skill,

playing with your pet, playing a game that you like,

coloring something you enjoy, cooking something new,

watching the documentaries to become more cultured,

keeping up with world events, volunteering your time,

attending church or spiritual practices, paying bills ontime,

paying down a credit card slowly on a daily basis...

Habit 1

"Let today be the day you give up who
you've been for who you can become."

- Hal Elrod

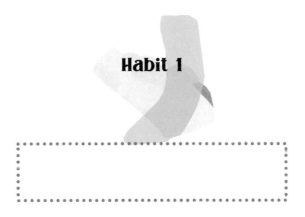

Habit 1

Known triggers: What events make you want to engage in this habit? What people, times of day, and moods cause you to practice this habit?

_____

_____

_____

_____

Preparation: What can you do to prepare for eliminating this habit for one month? (i.e. items you could buy to replace your habit with a healthier option, people to call who can hold you accountable, removing things from your house to have the habit out of reach, etc.)

_____

_____

_____

_____

Coping Mechanisms: What can you do instead when triggered to engage in this habit? Write several items or activities as well as people who can support you.

_____

_____

_____

_____

_____

Week 1: Write down what went right and what went wrong. List any and all triggers, old or new that you noticed, as well as how you coped or did not cope if you started to engage in the habit again. (Remember if you engaged, this is a moment to reflect and see how to get back on track as well as what you could do differently.)

_____

_____

_____

_____

_____

_____

_____

_____

_____

_____

_____

_____

Week 2: Write down what went right and what went wrong. List any and all triggers, old or new that you noticed, as well as how you coped or did not cope if you started to engage in the habit again. (Remember if you engaged, this is a moment to reflect and see how to get back on track as well as what you could do differently.)

_____

_____

_____

_____

_____

_____

_____

_____

_____

_____

_____

Week 3: Write down what went right and what went wrong. List any and all triggers, old or new that you noticed, as well as how you coped or did not cope if you started to engage in the habit again. (Remember if you engaged, this is a moment to reflect and see how to get back on track as well as what you could do differently.)

_____
_____
_____
_____
_____
_____
_____
_____
_____
_____
_____

Week 4: Write down what went right and what went wrong. List any and all triggers, old or new that you noticed, as well as how you coped or did not cope if you started to engage in the habit again. (Remember if you engaged, this is a moment to reflect and see how to get back on track as well as what you could do differently.)

_____
_____
_____
_____
_____
_____
_____
_____
_____
_____

End of Month Summary

Write down what you learned about yourself and this habit that you did not know at the beginning of this month. Discuss these insights and focus on your strengths and what changes you made for yourself.

_____

_____

_____

_____

_____

_____

_____

_____

_____

_____

_____

_____

_____

_____

_____

_____

_____

_____

_____

_____

_____

_____

_____

_____

Lastly, explore what your goal moving forward is for this habit. Do you want to continue to eliminate it from your life? Do you want to change to engaging in this habit a certain number of times per day/week/month that makes you feel more in control? Hold yourself accountable to your new goals for the following month and check back in to see how you did or if goals need to be revised again.

New Goal for this Habit Moving Forward:

Habit 2

"The chains of habit are too light to be felt until they
are too heavy to be broken."
-Samuel Johnson

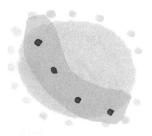

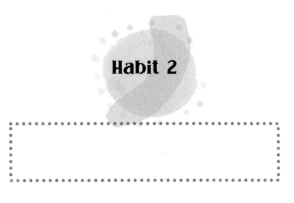

Habit 2

Known triggers: What events make you want to engage in this habit? What people, times of day, and moods cause you to practice this habit?

_____

_____

_____

_____

Preparation: What can you do to prepare for eliminating this habit for one month? (i.e. items you could buy to replace your habit with a healthier option, people to call who can hold you accountable, removing things from your house to have the habit out of reach, etc.)

_____

_____

_____

_____

Coping Mechanisms: What can you do instead when triggered to engage in this habit? Write several items or activities as well as people who can support you.

_____

_____

_____

_____

_____

_____

_____

Week 1: Write down what went right and what went wrong. List any and all triggers, old or new that you noticed, as well as how you coped or did not cope if you started to engage in the habit again. (Remember if you engaged, this is a moment to reflect and see how to get back on track as well as what you could do differently.)

_____

_____

_____

_____

_____

_____

_____

_____

_____

_____

_____

_____

Week 2: Write down what went right and what went wrong. List any and all triggers, old or new that you noticed, as well as how you coped or did not cope if you started to engage in the habit again. (Remember if you engaged, this is a moment to reflect and see how to get back on track as well as what you could do differently.)

_____

_____

_____

_____

_____

_____

_____

_____

_____

_____

_____

_____

Week 3: Write down what went right and what went wrong. List any and all triggers, old or new that you noticed, as well as how you coped or did not cope if you started to engage in the habit again. (Remember if you engaged, this is a moment to reflect and see how to get back on track as well as what you could do differently.)

_____

_____

_____

_____

_____

_____

_____

_____

_____

_____

_____

_____

Week 4: Write down what went right and what went wrong. List any and all triggers, old or new that you noticed, as well as how you coped or did not cope if you started to engage in the habit again. (Remember if you engaged, this is a moment to reflect and see how to get back on track as well as what you could do differently.)

_____

_____

_____

_____

_____

_____

_____

_____

_____

_____

End of Month Summary

Write down what you learned about yourself and this habit that you did not know at the beginning of this month. Discuss these insights and focus on your strengths and what changes you made for yourself.

_____

_____

_____

_____

_____

_____

_____

_____

_____

_____

_____

_____

_____

_____

_____

_____

_____

_____

_____

_____

_____

_____

_____

_____

_____

_____

_____

_____

_____

_____

Lastly, explore what your goal moving forward is for this habit. Do you want to continue to eliminate it from your life? Do you want to change to engaging in this habit a certain number of times per day/week/month that makes you feel more in control? Hold yourself accountable to your new goals for the following month and check back in to see how you did or if goals need to be revised again.

New Goal for this Habit Moving Forward:

Habit 3

"You'll never change your life until you change something you do daily. The secret of your success is found in our daily routine."
-John C. Maxwell

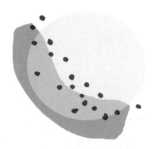

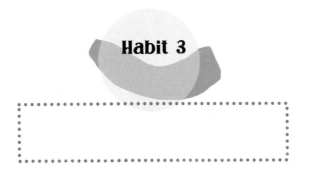

Habit 3

Known triggers: What events make you want to engage in this habit? What people, times of day, and moods cause you to practice this habit?

_____

_____

_____

_____

Preparation: What can you do to prepare for eliminating this habit for one month? (i.e. items you could buy to replace your habit with a healthier option, people to call who can hold you accountable, removing things from your house to have the habit out of reach, etc.)

_____

_____

_____

_____

Coping Mechanisms: What can you do instead when triggered to engage in this habit? Write several items or activities as well as people who can support you.

_____

_____

_____

_____

_____

_____

Week 1: Write down what went right and what went wrong. List any and all triggers, old or new that you noticed, as well as how you coped or did not cope if you started to engage in the habit again. (Remember if you engaged, this is a moment to reflect and see how to get back on track as well as what you could do differently.)

_____
_____
_____
_____
_____
_____
_____
_____
_____
_____
_____
_____
_____

Week 2: Write down what went right and what went wrong. List any and all triggers, old or new that you noticed, as well as how you coped or did not cope if you started to engage in the habit again. (Remember if you engaged, this is a moment to reflect and see how to get back on track as well as what you could do differently.)

_____
_____
_____
_____
_____
_____
_____
_____
_____
_____
_____
_____
_____

Week 3: Write down what went right and what went wrong. List any and all triggers, old or new that you noticed, as well as how you coped or did not cope if you started to engage in the habit again. (Remember if you engaged, this is a moment to reflect and see how to get back on track as well as what you could do differently.)

_____

_____

_____

_____

_____

_____

_____

_____

_____

_____

_____

Week 4: Write down what went right and what went wrong. List any and all triggers, old or new that you noticed, as well as how you coped or did not cope if you started to engage in the habit again. (Remember if you engaged, this is a moment to reflect and see how to get back on track as well as what you could do differently.)

_____

_____

_____

_____

_____

_____

_____

_____

_____

_____

_____

End of Month Summary

Write down what you learned about yourself and this habit that you did not know at the beginning of this month. Discuss these insights and focus on your strengths and what changes you made for yourself.

_____
_____
_____
_____
_____
_____
_____
_____
_____
_____
_____
_____
_____
_____
_____
_____
_____
_____
_____
_____
_____
_____
_____
_____
_____
_____
_____
_____
_____

Lastly, explore what your goal moving forward is for this habit. Do you want to continue to eliminate it from your life? Do you want to change to engaging in this habit a certain number of times per day/week/month that makes you feel more in control? Hold yourself accountable to your new goals for the following month and check back in to see how you did or if goals need to be revised again.

_____

_____

_____

_____

New Goal for this Habit Moving Forward:

_____

_____

Habit 4

"First forget inspiration. Habit is more dependable.
Habit will sustain you whether you're inspired or not."
-Octavia Butler

Habit 4

Known triggers: What events make you want to engage in this habit? What people, times of day, and moods cause you to practice this habit?

_____

_____

_____

_____

Preparation: What can you do to prepare for eliminating this habit for one month? (i.e. items you could buy to replace your habit with a healthier option, people to call who can hold you accountable, removing things from your house to have the habit out of reach, etc.)

_____

_____

_____

_____

Coping Mechanisms: What can you do instead when triggered to engage in this habit? Write several items or activities as well as people who can support you.

_____

_____

_____

_____

_____

_____

Week 1: Write down what went right and what went wrong. List any and all triggers, old or new that you noticed, as well as how you coped or did not cope if you started to engage in the habit again. (Remember if you engaged, this is a moment to reflect and see how to get back on track as well as what you could do differently.)

_____

_____

_____

_____

_____

_____

_____

_____

_____

_____

_____

_____

Week 2: Write down what went right and what went wrong. List any and all triggers, old or new that you noticed, as well as how you coped or did not cope if you started to engage in the habit again. (Remember if you engaged, this is a moment to reflect and see how to get back on track as well as what you could do differently.)

_____

_____

_____

_____

_____

_____

_____

_____

_____

_____

_____

Week 3: Write down what went right and what went wrong. List any and all triggers, old or new that you noticed, as well as how you coped or did not cope if you started to engage in the habit again. (Remember if you engaged, this is a moment to reflect and see how to get back on track as well as what you could do differently.)

_____

_____

_____

_____

_____

_____

_____

_____

_____

_____

_____

Week 4: Write down what went right and what went wrong. List any and all triggers, old or new that you noticed, as well as how you coped or did not cope if you started to engage in the habit again. (Remember if you engaged, this is a moment to reflect and see how to get back on track as well as what you could do differently.)

_____

_____

_____

_____

_____

_____

_____

_____

_____

_____

_____

End of Month Summary

Write down what you learned about yourself and this habit that you did not know at the beginning of this month. Discuss these insights and focus on your strengths and what changes you made for yourself.

_____

_____

_____

_____

_____

_____

_____

_____

_____

_____

_____

_____

_____

_____

_____

_____

_____

_____

_____

_____

_____

_____

_____

_____

_____

_____

_____

_____

_____

Lastly, explore what your goal moving forward is for this habit. Do you want to continue to eliminate it from your life? Do you want to change to engaging in this habit a certain number of times per day/week/month that makes you feel more in control? Hold yourself accountable to your new goals for the following month and check back in to see how you did or if goals need to be revised again.

_____

_____

_____

_____

_____

_____

_____

_____

_____

_____

_____

_____

_____

_____

_____

_____

_____

_____

_____

_____

_____

_____

New Goal for this Habit Moving Forward:

_____

_____

_____

Habit 5

"Habits change into character."
-Ovid

Habit 5

Known triggers: What events make you want to engage in this habit? What people, times of day, and moods cause you to practice this habit?

_____

_____

_____

_____

Preparation: What can you do to prepare for eliminating this habit for one month? (i.e. items you could buy to replace your habit with a healthier option, people to call who can hold you accountable, removing things from your house to have the habit out of reach, etc.)

_____

_____

_____

_____

Coping Mechanisms: What can you do instead when triggered to engage in this habit? Write several items or activities as well as people who can support you.

_____

_____

_____

_____

_____

_____

Week 1: Write down what went right and what went wrong. List any and all triggers, old or new that you noticed, as well as how you coped or did not cope if you started to engage in the habit again. (Remember if you engaged, this is a moment to reflect and see how to get back on track as well as what you could do differently.)

_____

_____

_____

_____

_____

_____

_____

_____

_____

_____

_____

Week 2: Write down what went right and what went wrong. List any and all triggers, old or new that you noticed, as well as how you coped or did not cope if you started to engage in the habit again. (Remember if you engaged, this is a moment to reflect and see how to get back on track as well as what you could do differently.)

_____

_____

_____

_____

_____

_____

_____

_____

_____

_____

_____

Week 3: Write down what went right and what went wrong. List any and all triggers, old or new that you noticed, as well as how you coped or did not cope if you started to engage in the habit again. (Remember if you engaged, this is a moment to reflect and see how to get back on track as well as what you could do differently.)

_____

_____

_____

_____

_____

_____

_____

_____

_____

_____

_____

Week 4: Write down what went right and what went wrong. List any and all triggers, old or new that you noticed, as well as how you coped or did not cope if you started to engage in the habit again. (Remember if you engaged, this is a moment to reflect and see how to get back on track as well as what you could do differently.)

_____

_____

_____

_____

_____

_____

_____

_____

_____

_____

_____

End of Month Summary

Write down what you learned about yourself and this habit that you did not know at the beginning of this month. Discuss these insights and focus on your strengths and what changes you made for yourself.

_____

_____

_____

_____

_____

_____

_____

_____

_____

_____

_____

_____

_____

_____

_____

_____

_____

_____

_____

_____

_____

_____

_____

_____

_____

_____

_____

_____

Lastly, explore what your goal moving forward is for this habit. Do you want to continue to eliminate it from your life? Do you want to change to engaging in this habit a certain number of times per day/week/month that makes you feel more in control? Hold yourself accountable to your new goals for the following month and check back in to see how you did or if goals need to be revised again.

_____

_____

_____

_____

_____

_____

_____

_____

_____

_____

_____

_____

_____

_____

_____

_____

_____

_____

_____

_____

_____

New Goal for this Habit Moving Forward:

_____

_____

_____

_____

Habit 6

"A habit cannot be tossed out the window; it must be coaxed down the stairs a step at a time."
-Mark Twain

Habit 6

Known triggers: What events make you want to engage in this habit? What people, times of day, and moods cause you to practice this habit?

_____

_____

_____

_____

Preparation: What can you do to prepare for eliminating this habit for one month? (i.e. items you could buy to replace your habit with a healthier option, people to call who can hold you accountable, removing things from your house to have the habit out of reach, etc.)

_____

_____

_____

_____

Coping Mechanisms: What can you do instead when triggered to engage in this habit? Write several items or activities as well as people who can support you.

_____

_____

_____

_____

_____

_____

Week 1: Write down what went right and what went wrong. List any and all triggers, old or new that you noticed, as well as how you coped or did not cope if you started to engage in the habit again. (Remember if you engaged, this is a moment to reflect and see how to get back on track as well as what you could do differently.)

_____

_____

_____

_____

_____

_____

_____

_____

_____

_____

_____

_____

Week 2: Write down what went right and what went wrong. List any and all triggers, old or new that you noticed, as well as how you coped or did not cope if you started to engage in the habit again. (Remember if you engaged, this is a moment to reflect and see how to get back on track as well as what you could do differently.)

_____

_____

_____

_____

_____

_____

_____

_____

_____

_____

_____

Week 3: Write down what went right and what went wrong. List any and all triggers, old or new that you noticed, as well as how you coped or did not cope if you started to engage in the habit again. (Remember if you engaged, this is a moment to reflect and see how to get back on track as well as what you could do differently.)

_____

_____

_____

_____

_____

_____

_____

_____

_____

_____

_____

Week 4: Write down what went right and what went wrong. List any and all triggers, old or new that you noticed, as well as how you coped or did not cope if you started to engage in the habit again. (Remember if you engaged, this is a moment to reflect and see how to get back on track as well as what you could do differently.)

_____

_____

_____

_____

_____

_____

_____

_____

_____

_____

_____

End of Month Summary

Write down what you learned about yourself and this habit that you did not know at the beginning of this month. Discuss these insights and focus on your strengths and what changes you made for yourself.

Lastly, explore what your goal moving forward is for this habit. Do you want to continue to eliminate it from your life? Do you want to change to engaging in this habit a certain number of times per day/week/month that makes you feel more in control? Hold yourself accountable to your new goals for the following month and check back in to see how you did or if goals need to be revised again.

New Goal for this Habit Moving Forward:

Habit 7

"If you are going to achieve excellence in big things, you develop the habit in little matters. Excellence is not an exception, it is a prevailing attitude."
-Colin Powell

Habit 7

Choose a habit to either eliminate if you still have habits you wish
to get rid of or choose a habit to ADD to make your life better.

Known triggers: What events make you want to engage in this habit or avoid
adding the good habit? What people, what times of day might be difficult for you,
what moods cause you to do or avoid doing this habit?

_____

_____

_____

_____

Preparation: What can you do to prepare for eliminating or adding this habit for
one month? (i.e. items you could buy to replace or make engagement in this habit
easier, people to call to hold you accountable, removing or adding things to your
house to have habit in or out of reach, etc).

_____

_____

_____

_____

Coping Mechanisms: What can you do instead when triggered to engage in this
habit? Or what can you do to help yourself want to engage in the new added
habit? Write several items or activities as well as people who can support you.

_____

_____

_____

_____

Week 1: Write down what went right and what went wrong. List any and all triggers, old or new that you noticed, as well as how you coped or did not cope if you started to engage ior didn't start to add in the habit again. (Remember if you skipped a day, this is a moment to reflect and see how to get back on track as well as what you could do differently.)

_____
_____
_____
_____
_____
_____
_____
_____
_____
_____
_____
_____

Week 2: Write down what went right and what went wrong. List any and all triggers, old or new that you noticed, as well as how you coped or did not cope if you started to engage or didn't start to ad in the habit again. (Remember if you skipped a day, this is a moment to reflect and see how to get back on track as well as what you could do differently.)

_____
_____
_____
_____
_____
_____
_____
_____
_____
_____
_____
_____

Week 3: Write down what went right and what went wrong. List any and all triggers, old or new that you noticed, as well as how you coped or did not cope if you started to engage or didn't start to ad in the habit again. (Remember if you skipped a day, this is a moment to reflect and see how to get back on track as well as what you could do differently.)

Week 4: Write down what went right and what went wrong. List any and all triggers, old or new that you noticed, as well as how you coped or did not cope if you started to engage or didn't start to ad in the habit again. (Remember if you skipped a day, this is a moment to reflect and see how to get back on track as well as what you could do differently.)

End of Month Summary

Write down what you learned about yourself and this habit that you did not know at the beginning of this month. Discuss these insights and focus on your strengths and what changes you made for yourself.

_____

_____

_____

_____

_____

_____

_____

_____

_____

_____

_____

_____

_____

_____

_____

_____

_____

_____

_____

_____

_____

_____

_____

_____

_____

_____

Lastly, explore what your goal moving forward is for this habit. Do you want to continue to eliminate or add it daily for your life? Do you want to change to engaging in this habit a certain number of times per day/week/month that makes you feel more in control? Hold yourself accountable to your new goals for the following month and check back in to see how you did or if goals need to be revised again.

New Goal for this Habit Moving Forward:

Habit 8

"The world as we have created it is a process of our thinking. It cannot be changed without changing our thinking."
-Albert Einstein

Habit 8

Choose a habit to either eliminate if you still have habits you wish
to get rid of or choose a habit to ADD to make your life better.

Known triggers: What events make you want to engage in this habit or avoid
adding the good habit? What people, what times of day might be difficult for you,
what moods cause you to do or avoid doing this habit?

_____

_____

_____

_____

Preparation: What can you do to prepare for eliminating or adding this habit for
one month? (i.e. items you could buy to replace or make engagement in this habit
easier, people to call to hold you accountable, removing or adding things to your
house to have habit in or out of reach, etc).

_____

_____

_____

Coping Mechanisms: What can you do instead when triggered to engage in this
habit? Or what can you do to help yourself want to engage in the new added
habit? Write several items or activities as well as people who can support you.

_____

_____

_____

_____

Week 1: Write down what went right and what went wrong. List any and all triggers, old or new that you noticed, as well as how you coped or did not cope if you started to engage ior didn't start to add in the habit again. (Remember if you skipped a day, this is a moment to reflect and see how to get back on track as well as what you could do differently.)

_____

_____

_____

_____

_____

_____

_____

_____

_____

_____

Week 2: Write down what went right and what went wrong. List any and all triggers, old or new that you noticed, as well as how you coped or did not cope if you started to engage or didn't start to ad in the habit again. (Remember if you skipped a day, this is a moment to reflect and see how to get back on track as well as what you could do differently.)

_____

_____

_____

_____

_____

_____

_____

_____

_____

_____

_____

Week 3: Write down what went right and what went wrong. List any and all triggers, old or new that you noticed, as well as how you coped or did not cope if you started to engage or didn't start to ad in the habit again. (Remember if you skipped a day, this is a moment to reflect and see how to get back on track as well as what you could do differently.)

Week 4: Write down what went right and what went wrong. List any and all triggers, old or new that you noticed, as well as how you coped or did not cope if you started to engage or didn't start to ad in the habit again. (Remember if you skipped a day, this is a moment to reflect and see how to get back on track as well as what you could do differently.)

End of Month Summary

Write down what you learned about yourself and this habit that you did not know at the beginning of this month. Discuss these insights and focus on your strengths and what changes you made for yourself.

_____

_____

_____

_____

_____

_____

_____

_____

_____

_____

_____

_____

_____

_____

_____

_____

_____

_____

_____

_____

_____

_____

_____

_____

_____

_____

Lastly, explore what your goal moving forward is for this habit. Do you want to continue to eliminate or add it daily for your life? Do you want to change to engaging in this habit a certain number of times per day/week/month that makes you feel more in control? Hold yourself accountable to your new goals for the following month and check back in to see how you did or if goals need to be revised again.

_____

_____

_____

_____

_____

_____

_____

_____

_____

_____

_____

_____

_____

_____

_____

_____

_____

_____

_____

_____

New Goal for this Habit Moving Forward:

_____

_____

_____

_____

Habit 9

"Drop by drop is the water pot filled."
-Buddha

Habit 9

Choose a habit to either eliminate if you still have habits you wish to get rid of or choose a habit to ADD to make your life better.

Known triggers: What events make you want to engage in this habit or avoid adding the good habit? What people, what times of day might be difficult for you, what moods cause you to do or avoid doing this habit?

_____

_____

_____

_____

Preparation: What can you do to prepare for eliminating or adding this habit for one month? (i.e. items you could buy to replace or make engagement in this habit easier, people to call to hold you accountable, removing or adding things to your house to have habit in or out of reach, etc).

_____

_____

_____

_____

Coping Mechanisms: What can you do instead when triggered to engage in this habit? Or what can you do to help yourself want to engage in the new added habit? Write several items or activities as well as people who can support you.

_____

_____

_____

_____

Week 1: Write down what went right and what went wrong. List any and all triggers, old or new that you noticed, as well as how you coped or did not cope if you started to engage ior didn't start to add in the habit again. (Remember if you skipped a day, this is a moment to reflect and see how to get back on track as well as what you could do differently.)

_____

_____

_____

_____

_____

_____

_____

_____

_____

_____

Week 2: Write down what went right and what went wrong. List any and all triggers, old or new that you noticed, as well as how you coped or did not cope if you started to engage or didn't start to ad in the habit again. (Remember if you skipped a day, this is a moment to reflect and see how to get back on track as well as what you could do differently.)

_____

_____

_____

_____

_____

_____

_____

_____

_____

_____

Week 3: Write down what went right and what went wrong. List any and all triggers, old or new that you noticed, as well as how you coped or did not cope if you started to engage or didn't start to ad in the habit again. (Remember if you skipped a day, this is a moment to reflect and see how to get back on track as well as what you could do differently.)

_____
_____
_____
_____
_____
_____
_____
_____
_____
_____

Week 4: Write down what went right and what went wrong. List any and all triggers, old or new that you noticed, as well as how you coped or did not cope if you started to engage or didn't start to ad in the habit again. (Remember if you skipped a day, this is a moment to reflect and see how to get back on track as well as what you could do differently.)

_____
_____
_____
_____
_____
_____
_____
_____
_____
_____
_____

End of Month Summary

Write down what you learned about yourself and this habit that you did not know at the beginning of this month. Discuss these insights and focus on your strengths and what changes you made for yourself.

_____

_____

_____

_____

_____

_____

_____

_____

_____

_____

_____

_____

_____

_____

_____

_____

_____

_____

_____

_____

_____

_____

_____

_____

_____

_____

_____

_____

Lastly, explore what your goal moving forward is for this habit. Do you want to continue to eliminate or add it daily for your life? Do you want to change to engaging in this habit a certain number of times per day/week/month that makes you feel more in control? Hold yourself accountable to your new goals for the following month and check back in to see how you did or if goals need to be revised again.

_____

New Goal for this Habit Moving Forward:

Habit 10

"I now tried a new hypothesis: It was possible that I was more in charge of my happiness than I was allowing myself to be."
–Michelle Obama

Habit 10

Choose a habit to either eliminate if you still have habits you wish
to get rid of or choose a habit to ADD to make your life better.

Known triggers: What events make you want to engage in this habit or avoid
adding the good habit? What people, what times of day might be difficult for you,
what moods cause you to do or avoid doing this habit?

_____

_____

_____

_____

Preparation: What can you do to prepare for eliminating or adding this habit for
one month? (i.e. items you could buy to replace or make engagement in this habit
easier, people to call to hold you accountable, removing or adding things to your
house to have habit in or out of reach, etc).

_____

_____

_____

_____

Coping Mechanisms: What can you do instead when triggered to engage in this
habit? Or what can you do to help yourself want to engage in the new added
habit? Write several items or activities as well as people who can support you.

_____

_____

_____

_____

Week 1: Write down what went right and what went wrong. List any and all triggers, old or new that you noticed, as well as how you coped or did not cope if you started to engage ior didn't start to add in the habit again. (Remember if you skipped a day, this is a moment to reflect and see how to get back on track as well as what you could do differently.)

_____

_____

_____

_____

_____

_____

_____

_____

_____

_____

Week 2: Write down what went right and what went wrong. List any and all triggers, old or new that you noticed, as well as how you coped or did not cope if you started to engage or didn't start to ad in the habit again. (Remember if you skipped a day, this is a moment to reflect and see how to get back on track as well as what you could do differently.)

_____

_____

_____

_____

_____

_____

_____

_____

_____

_____

Week 3: Write down what went right and what went wrong. List any and all triggers, old or new that you noticed, as well as how you coped or did not cope if you started to engage or didn't start to ad in the habit again. (Remember if you skipped a day, this is a moment to reflect and see how to get back on track as well as what you could do differently.)

_____

_____

_____

_____

_____

_____

_____

_____

_____

_____

_____

Week 4: Write down what went right and what went wrong. List any and all triggers, old or new that you noticed, as well as how you coped or did not cope if you started to engage or didn't start to ad in the habit again. (Remember if you skipped a day, this is a moment to reflect and see how to get back on track as well as what you could do differently.)

_____

_____

_____

_____

_____

_____

_____

_____

_____

_____

_____

End of Month Summary

Write down what you learned about yourself and this habit that you did not know at the beginning of this month. Discuss these insights and focus on your strengths and what changes you made for yourself.

_____

_____

_____

_____

_____

_____

_____

_____

_____

_____

_____

_____

_____

_____

_____

_____

_____

_____

_____

_____

_____

_____

_____

_____

_____

_____

_____

Lastly, explore what your goal moving forward is for this habit. Do you want to continue to eliminate or add it daily for your life? Do you want to change to engaging in this habit a certain number of times per day/week/month that makes you feel more in control? Hold yourself accountable to your new goals for the following month and check back in to see how you did or if goals need to be revised again.

New Goal for this Habit Moving Forward:

Habit 11

"Successful people are simply those with
successful habits."
-Brian Tracy

Habit 11

Choose a habit to either eliminate if you still have habits you wish
to get rid of or choose a habit to ADD to make your life better.

Known triggers: What events make you want to engage in this habit or avoid
adding the good habit? What people, what times of day might be difficult for you,
what moods cause you to do or avoid doing this habit?

_____

_____

_____

_____

Preparation: What can you do to prepare for eliminating or adding this habit for
one month? (i.e. items you could buy to replace or make engagement in this habit
easier, people to call to hold you accountable, removing or adding things to your
house to have habit in or out of reach, etc).

_____

_____

_____

_____

Coping Mechanisms: What can you do instead when triggered to engage in this
habit? Or what can you do to help yourself want to engage in the new added
habit? Write several items or activities as well as people who can support you.

_____

_____

_____

_____

Week 1: Write down what went right and what went wrong. List any and all triggers, old or new that you noticed, as well as how you coped or did not cope if you started to engage ior didn't start to add in the habit again. (Remember if you skipped a day, this is a moment to reflect and see how to get back on track as well as what you could do differently.)

_____
_____
_____
_____
_____
_____
_____
_____
_____
_____
_____

Week 2: Write down what went right and what went wrong. List any and all triggers, old or new that you noticed, as well as how you coped or did not cope if you started to engage or didn't start to ad in the habit again. (Remember if you skipped a day, this is a moment to reflect and see how to get back on track as well as what you could do differently.)

_____
_____
_____
_____
_____
_____
_____
_____
_____
_____
_____

Week 3: Write down what went right and what went wrong. List any and all triggers, old or new that you noticed, as well as how you coped or did not cope if you started to engage or didn't start to ad in the habit again. (Remember if you skipped a day, this is a moment to reflect and see how to get back on track as well as what you could do differently.)

_____

_____

_____

_____

_____

_____

_____

_____

_____

_____

_____

_____

Week 4: Write down what went right and what went wrong. List any and all triggers, old or new that you noticed, as well as how you coped or did not cope if you started to engage or didn't start to ad in the habit again. (Remember if you skipped a day, this is a moment to reflect and see how to get back on track as well as what you could do differently.)

_____

_____

_____

_____

_____

_____

_____

_____

_____

_____

_____

_____

End of Month Summary

Write down what you learned about yourself and this habit that you did not know at the beginning of this month. Discuss these insights and focus on your strengths and what changes you made for yourself.

_____

_____

_____

_____

_____

_____

_____

_____

_____

_____

_____

_____

_____

_____

_____

_____

_____

_____

_____

_____

_____

_____

_____

_____

_____

_____

_____

_____

Lastly, explore what your goal moving forward is for this habit. Do you want to continue to eliminate or add it daily for your life? Do you want to change to engaging in this habit a certain number of times per day/week/month that makes you feel more in control? Hold yourself accountable to your new goals for the following month and check back in to see how you did or if goals need to be revised again.

New Goal for this Habit Moving Forward:

Habit 12

"Happiness is not something ready made.
It comes from your own actions."
- Dalai Lama XIV

Habit 12

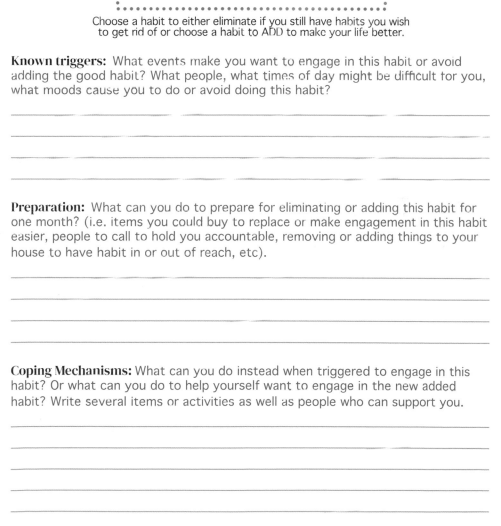

Choose a habit to either eliminate if you still have habits you wish
to get rid of or choose a habit to ADD to make your life better.

Known triggers: What events make you want to engage in this habit or avoid
adding the good habit? What people, what times of day might be difficult for you,
what moods cause you to do or avoid doing this habit?

_____

_____

_____

_____

Preparation: What can you do to prepare for eliminating or adding this habit for
one month? (i.e. items you could buy to replace or make engagement in this habit
easier, people to call to hold you accountable, removing or adding things to your
house to have habit in or out of reach, etc).

_____

_____

_____

_____

Coping Mechanisms: What can you do instead when triggered to engage in this
habit? Or what can you do to help yourself want to engage in the new added
habit? Write several items or activities as well as people who can support you.

_____

_____

_____

_____

Week 1: Write down what went right and what went wrong. List any and all triggers, old or new that you noticed, as well as how you coped or did not cope if you started to engage ior didn't start to add in the habit again. (Remember if you skipped a day, this is a moment to reflect and see how to get back on track as well as what you could do differently.)

_____

_____

_____

_____

_____

_____

_____

_____

_____

_____

_____

Week 2: Write down what went right and what went wrong. List any and all triggers, old or new that you noticed, as well as how you coped or did not cope if you started to engage or didn't start to ad in the habit again. (Remember if you skipped a day, this is a moment to reflect and see how to get back on track as well as what you could do differently.)

_____

_____

_____

_____

_____

_____

_____

_____

_____

_____

_____

Week 3: Write down what went right and what went wrong. List any and all triggers, old or new that you noticed, as well as how you coped or did not cope if you started to engage or didn't start to ad in the habit again. (Remember if you skipped a day, this is a moment to reflect and see how to get back on track as well as what you could do differently.)

_____

_____

_____

_____

_____

_____

_____

_____

_____

_____

_____

_____

Week 4: Write down what went right and what went wrong. List any and all triggers, old or new that you noticed, as well as how you coped or did not cope if you started to engage or didn't start to ad in the habit again. (Remember if you skipped a day, this is a moment to reflect and see how to get back on track as well as what you could do differently.)

_____

_____

_____

_____

_____

_____

_____

_____

_____

_____

_____

_____

End of Month Summary

Write down what you learned about yourself and this habit that you did not know at the beginning of this month. Discuss these insights and focus on your strengths and what changes you made for yourself.

_____

_____

_____

_____

_____

_____

_____

_____

_____

_____

_____

_____

_____

_____

_____

_____

_____

_____

_____

_____

_____

_____

_____

_____

_____

_____

_____

_____

Lastly, explore what your goal moving forward is for this habit. Do you want to continue to eliminate or add it daily for your life? Do you want to change to engaging in this habit a certain number of times per day/week/month that makes you feel more in control? Hold yourself accountable to your new goals for the following month and check back in to see how you did or if goals need to be revised again.

New Goal for this Habit Moving Forward:

Summary

"And once you understand that habits can change,
you have the freedom and the responsibility
to remake them."
-Charles Duhigg

End of Year Summary

What you learn about your habits over the past year?

_____

_____

_____

_____

_____

_____

_____

_____

_____

_____

What did you learn this past year ? Strengths? Weaknesses?

_____

_____

_____

_____

_____

_____

_____

_____

_____

_____

_____

_____

What do you want your goals related to by 12 habits to be moving forward?

_____

_____

_____

_____

_____

_____

_____

_____

_____

_____

_____

_____

_____

_____

_____

_____

_____

_____

_____

_____

_____

_____

_____

_____

_____

_____

_____

_____

_____

_____

Any additional thoughts for yourselff?

Kendal Maxwell, Ph.D., is a Clinical Neuropsychologist at an academic medical center in Los Angeles, CA providing brief psychotherapeutic interventions and assessments to her clients. She also is the lead neuropsychologist within the Amyotrophic Lateral Sclerosis (ALS) clinic at said center and practices a combination of interventions from Cognitive Behavioral Therapy as well Existential Therapy and Acceptance Commitment based therapy models with her clients. Additionally, she is the author of two podcast series, *21 Day Positive Mindfulness Meditation Challenge* and *21 Day Acceptance Meditation Challenge*, one of which has over 1 million downloads and reaches audiences worldwide. Additionally, she enjoys reaching lay audiences daily by providing "Mini Meditations" and research in psychology through her Tiktok and Instagram @positivemindmediator.

She lives in Los Angeles, California.

"We need to accept that we won't always make the right decisions, that we'll screw up royally sometimes – understanding that failure is not the opposite of success, it's part of success."
– Arianna Huffington

While using this journal, you may encounter strong emotions that require assistance from a therapist. Additionally, this journal may not be suitable for individuals with substance use disorders in need of help reducing their use with assistance from a medical and/or psychiatric team. Below are some potential resources for you if in need of additional help or psychological support and can be accessed within the United States. If you are in immediate danger to yourself or others, please call 911.

- Suicide & Crisis Lifeline: text 988 in the United States for voice or text options

- The American Foundation for Suicide Prevention provides referrals to support groups and mental health professionals, resources on loss, and suicide prevention information (1-888-333-2377)

- National Eating Disorder Association: 1-800-931-2237.

- National Alliance on Mental Illness: 1-800-950-6264 or Text HOME to 741741 for 24/7 crisis counseling.

- Substance Abuse and Mental Health Services Administration (SAMHSA)'s National Helpline, 1-800-662-HELP (4357), (also known as the Treatment Referral Routing Service) or TTY: 1-800-487-4889 is a confidential, free, 24-hour a-day, 365-day-a-year, information service, in English and Spanish, for individuals and family members facing mental and/or substance use disorders. This service provides referrals to local treatment facilities, support groups, and community-based organizations. Callers can also order free publications and other information.

- Veterans Crisis Line: 1-800-273-8255 and press 1 or Text: 838255. Available 24/7, confidential and serves all Veterans, service members, national guard and reserve, as well as their family members and friends.

- Disaster Distress Helpline Call or text 1-800-985-5990
The disaster distress helpline provides immediate crisis counseling for people who are experiencing emotional distress related to any natural or human-caused disaster. The helpline is free, multilingual, confidential, and available 24 hours a day, seven days a week.

- Depression and Bipolar Support Alliance: www.dbsalliance.org provides information on bipolar disorder and depression, offers in-person and online support groups and forums (1-800-826-3632)

- International OCD Foundation provides information on OCD and treatment referrals (1-617-973-5801) http://iocdf.org/

- Children and Adults with Attention-Deficit/Hyperactivity Disorder (CHADD) provides information and referrals on ADHD, including local support groups (1-800-233-4050). www.chadd.org

- Schizophrenia and Related Disorders Alliance of America (SARDAA) offers Schizophrenia Anonymous self-help groups and toll-free teleconferences (1-240-423-9432). www.sardaa.org

- Psychology Today offers a national directory of therapists, psychiatrists, therapy groups and treatment facility options. Filters are available to search by insurance taken as well as specialties of providers. www.psychologytoday.com